EDGE BOOKS

EQUIPPED FOR BATTLE

WEAPONS, GEAR, AND UNIFORMS

★ OF ★

WORLD WAR I

by Eric Fein

Consultant:
Jennifer L. Jones
Chair, Armed Forces History
NMAH, Smithsonian Institution
Washington, D.C.

CAPSTONE PRESS
a capstone imprint

Edge Books are published by Capstone Press,
1710 Roe Crest Drive, North Mankato, Minnesota 56003.
www.capstonepub.com

 Books published by Capstone Press are manufactured with paper
containing at least 10 percent post-consumer waste.

Library of Congress Cataloging-in-Publication Data
Fein, Eric.
   Weapons, gear, and uniforms of World War I / by Eric Fein.
   p. cm.—(Edge books. Equipped for battle)
   Includes bibliographical references and index.
   Summary: "Describes the uniforms, gear, and weapons used by the Central Powers
and Allied Powers during World War I"—Provided by publisher.
   Audience: Grades 4-6.
   ISBN 978-1-4296-7649-6 (library binding)
   1. World War, 1914–1918—Equipment and supplies—Juvenile literature.
2. Military weapons—History—20th century—Juvenile literature. I. Title. II. Series.
D522.7.F46 2012
940.4'83—dc23   2011028686

Editorial Credits

Aaron Sautter, editor; Ted Williams, designer; Eric Manske, production specialist

Photo Credits

Alamy: akg-images, 10 (top), 23 (bottom), Dorling Kindersley, 17 (bottom),
INTERFOTO, 10 (bottom), 18 (top), Photos 12/Oasis, cover (soldier); Corbis, 21 (top),
23 (top), Bettmann, 13 (top), 14 (top), 25 (top), 28 (top), Dazo Vintage Stock Photos/
Images.com, 9 (left), Hulton-Deutsch Collection, 4-5, 8, 11 (bottom), 14 (bottom), 22,
26, 27 (bottom); Getty Images: Archive Photos/George Eastman House, 25 (middle),
Hulton Archive, 12, 24, 29, Hulton Archive/Three Lions, 25 (bottom), Hulton Archive/
Topical Press Agency, 27 (top), Imagno, 11 (top), Mansell/Time Life Pictures, 28 (bottom),
Popperfoto/Paul Popper, cover (battle); Newscom: akg-images, 21 (bottom), Central
News/Mirrorpix, 15, Official Photograph of the Australia Commonwealth/Mirrorpix, 13
(bottom); Shutterstock: BESTWEB, 18 (bottom),Olemac, cover (gun), 17 (middle); Super
Stock Inc./Science and Society, 9 (right); Wikimedia, 19 (top), Antique Military Rifles, 17
(top); www.historicalimagebank.com, 16, 19 (bottom), 20 (bottom),Connecticut History
Museum, 20 (top)

Artistic Effects

Shutterstock: Ewa Walicka, Jim Barber, Kurt De Bruyn, maigi,
osov, Supertrooper

Printed in the United States of America in Stevens Point, Wisconsin.

102011   006404WZS12

TABLE OF CONTENTS

THE WAR TO
★ END ALL WARS ★

The early 1900s saw a lot of tension among countries in Europe. Britain, France, and Germany all wanted to be the most powerful nation in the world. Austria-Hungary and Russia competed to control parts of eastern Europe. And the United States was also growing into a world power. The friction between countries eventually led to events that would erupt into war.

World War I (1914–1918) began with the **assassination** of Austria's Archduke Franz Ferdinand. Austria accused Serbia of a plot to murder him. Other nations quickly took sides. Germany supported Austria. Russia, France, and Great Britain came to the defense of Serbia. The United States did not join the war until 1917. But U.S. forces helped determine the war's outcome.

assassination—the murder of someone who is well known or important

Most nations thought the war would be short. But it turned into one of the longest and costliest wars ever fought. Bloody battles raged across Europe, the Middle East, Africa, and Asia for four years.

Armies began using several new weapons during the war. Tanks were widely used in war for the first time. Soldiers on both sides feared deadly new gas weapons. More than 37 million soldiers were killed, wounded, or went missing during the war. The horrific fighting led the conflict to be called "The War to End All Wars."

ATLANTIC OCEAN

IRELAND

Bay of Biscay

PORTUGAL

SPAIN

MOROCCO

FOUR MAJOR WORLD WAR I BATTLES

◉ FIRST BATTLE OF YPRES

Fought: October 18, 1914–November 22, 1914
Allied Powers casualties: about 160,000
Central Powers casualties: about 130,000

◯ GALLIPOLI CAMPAIGN

Fought: April 25, 1915–January 9, 1916
Allied Powers casualties: more than 280,000
Central Powers casualties: about 250,000

◉ BATTLE OF VERDUN

Fought: February 21, 1916–December 18, 1916
Allied Powers casualties: about 370,000
Central Powers casualties: about 340,000

◉ BATTLE OF THE SOMME

Fought: July 1, 1916–November 18, 1916
Allied Powers casualties: more than 620,000
Central Powers casualties: about 500,000

ALLIED AND CENTRAL POWERS IN EUROPE, 1914

NORWAY

SWEDEN

Gulf of Finland

North Sea

DENMARK

Baltic Sea

N

W   E

S

UNITED KINGDOM

NETH.

BELGIUM

GERMAN EMPIRE

RUSSIA

AUSTRIA-HUNGARY

SWITZERLAND

FRANCE

ITALY

Adriatic Sea

ROMANIA

Black Sea

SERBIA

BULGARIA

MONTENEGRO

ALBANIA

GREECE

OTTOMAN EMPIRE

Aegean Sea

Tyrrhenian Sea

...terranean Sea

Ionian Sea

...ERIA

TUNISIA

	ALLIED POWERS
	CENTRAL POWERS
	NEUTRAL NATIONS

★ UNIFORMS ★

At the beginning of World War I, some armies dressed their soldiers in brightly colored uniforms. The colorful clothing made it easier for soldiers to see one another on the battlefield. But that soon changed after fighting broke out in Europe. Being hard to see on a battlefield became a matter of survival.

ALLIED POWERS UNIFORMS

FRENCH UNIFORMS

At the start of the war, French soldiers wore brightly colored uniforms. Their clothes included a dark blue overcoat, red pants, and flat-topped kepi hats. But by May 1915, they began wearing standard blue uniforms that were harder for the enemy to spot.

RUSSIAN UNIFORMS

Russian soldiers wore light olive-green uniforms and a peaked cap. They also wore heavy hats during winter. The hats had flaps that could be used to cover soldiers' ears and necks. Rough wool greatcoats could also be used as cloaks or blankets.

BRITISH UNIFORMS

British soldiers wore basic khaki uniforms. The uniforms included single-breasted tunics with folding collars. There were also pants, **puttees**, and ankle boots. The khaki peaked cap sometimes had ear and neck flaps.

U.S. UNIFORMS

U.S. soldiers also wore khaki uniforms. An overseas cap was issued to troops sent to other countries. But when soldiers faced battle, they wore steel helmets and gas masks instead.

BATTLE FACT

Some Scottish troops went into battle wearing kilts. These heavy, knee-length wool skirts were usually made with a plaid pattern woven into them.

 puttee—a strip of cloth wound around a soldier's leg from ankle to knee as part of a uniform

CENTRAL POWERS UNIFORMS

GERMAN UNIFORMS

German soldiers wore gray-green uniforms that included a single-breasted tunic with eight buttons. The pants were worn with knee boots. At the start of the war, German soldiers wore spiked helmets made of leather. But by 1916 these helmets were replaced with steel helmets that did a better job of protecting soldiers from **shrapnel**.

GERMAN HELMETS WITH STEEL BROW PLATES

German soldiers with very dangerous jobs had a steel plate strapped to the front of their helmets. These brow plates gave soldiers added protection, but were very heavy. The helmet and plate combined weighed more than 13 pounds (5.9 kilograms).

OTTOMAN EMPIRE UNIFORMS

Turkish soldiers from the Ottoman Empire wore German-style uniforms that were a greenish-khaki color. They included a single-breasted tunic with a folding collar, breeches, and puttees.

 shrapnel—pieces that have broken off from an explosive shell

AUSTRO-HUNGARIAN UNIFORMS

When the war began, the Austro-Hungarian army wore blue-gray uniforms. However, by 1916 the uniforms changed to be similar to those worn by the German military.

ROYAL HUNGARIAN ARMY UNIFORMS

These uniforms were very similar to regular Austro-Hungarian soldiers' clothes. However, the belt buckle had the Hungarian coat of arms. The long tight-fitting pants also had Hungarian knots on the thighs and braiding down the outside seam.

BULGARIAN UNIFORMS

Bulgarian soldiers wore gray-green uniforms that looked similar to Russian uniforms. However, because of shortages, they were not worn by all soldiers. Some wore German uniforms. Bulgarian soldiers sometimes wore caps with a black or gray-green leather peak and chin strap.

TRENCH WARFARE

Across much of Europe, soldiers on both sides lived and fought in deep trenches. Life in the trenches was a nightmare. Rats and filthy water constantly led to diseases. Poison gas was first used as part of trench warfare. To survive the deadly gas, armies on both sides carried gas masks for protection.

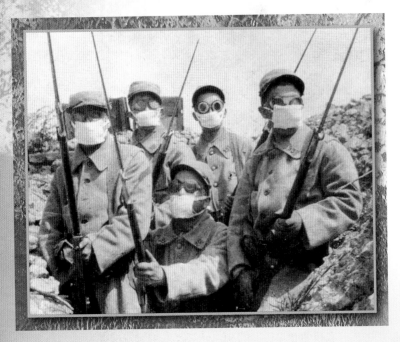

EARLY GAS MASKS

Early French and British gas masks were basically goggles and a gauze pad. Later, flannel hoods with eyepieces were used.

WIRE CUTTERS

Barbed wire often covered the area between opposing trenches, which was known as "no-man's-land." Soldiers used wire cutters to cut through the wire and cross over this area. There were several kinds of wire cutters. They included folding cutters and cutters that fit on the barrel of a rifle.

GERMAN GAS MASKS

German gas masks were made from rubber-coated cloth or oiled leather. They were hot and uncomfortable to wear. They also didn't protect soldiers well against large amounts of gas.

SMALL BOX RESPIRATORS

These British gas masks had shatterproof eyepieces. Special valves allowed soldiers to breath without making the eyepieces fog up. The masks protected soldiers from all gases except mustard gas.

BATTLE FACT
The Germans launched the first gas attack of the war on April 22, 1915, at Ypres, Belgium.

TRENCH PERISCOPES

Handheld periscopes were an important tool for soldiers fighting in trenches. Periscopes allowed soldiers to watch their enemies while staying protected in the trenches.

PORTABLE FIELD TELEPHONES

Portable field telephones were often carried in a leather shoulder bag. The phone came with keys used for sending Morse code. Morse code was used when soldiers were in battle and couldn't hear the speaker at the other end of the phone.

CARRIER PIGEONS

Sometimes, trained pigeons were the only way soldiers on the front lines could communicate with headquarters. Soldiers tied messages to the pigeons' legs and then sent them back to commanding officers.

BATTLE FACT

France gave the Legion of Honor award to a carrier pigeon. The bird had carried out its mission after being exposed to poison gas. It died soon after it delivered the message.

DOG MESSENGERS

Dogs were often used to carry messages between trenches. The messages were kept in tubes on the dogs' collars. The dogs were trained to leap over barbed wire. The dogs ran fast and were hard for snipers to shoot.

STAR SHELLS

Star shells were magnesium flares that burned brightly when fired into the air. They were used as prearranged signals. The shells were different colors, and each had a specific meaning. The shells also provided light in no-man's-land so enemy movements could be seen at night.

MESS KITS

Soldiers usually carried mess kits for eating their meals. A kit included a cup, a spoon, and a fork. Some kits also had containers to hold alcohol and chocolate rations.

Rifles and handguns became much more accurate and reliable during the war. Many of the rifles used by warring nations were similar in their basic designs. The rifles used **magazines** and bolt-action loading systems. These systems could eject a used shell and load a new one at the same time. This design allowed soldiers to keep firing without manually reloading their rifles.

RIFLES

SPRINGFIELD RIFLES

U.S. soldiers mainly used 1903 Springfield rifles. These guns could fire bullets at 2,700 feet (823 meters) per second. The gun came with a five-round clip, weighed 8.5 pounds (3.9 kg), and was 3.6 feet (1.1 m) long. It was one of the lightest and shortest rifles used in the war.

LEBEL 1893 MODEL RIFLES

The French army used the Lebel 1893 rifle. Its magazine held eight rounds. The Lebel was the heaviest of all the rifles used in the war. It weighed 9.2 pounds (4.2 kg) and measured 4.3 feet (1.3 m) long.

★ **magazine**—a metal or plastic case that holds bullets and fits inside a gun

MODEL 1891 MOSIN-NAGANT RIFLES

The 1891 Mosin-Nagant weighed 9 pounds (4.1 kg) and was 4.3 feet (1.3 m) long. It was very popular with Russian troops. Russian factories produced 111,000 of these rifles a month, but it still wasn't enough to meet demand.

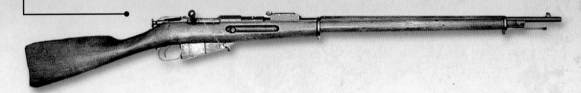

MODEL 1898 MAUSER RIFLES

German 1898 Mauser rifles were longer and heavier than British and U.S. rifles. They were 4.1 feet (1.2 m) long and weighed about 9 pounds (4.1 kg).

GERMAN ANTI-TANK RIFLES

Nicknamed the "elephant gun," this anti-tank rifle was developed by Germany. The 13.3 mm rounds could pierce armor up to 1.2 inches (3 centimeters) thick. The rifle weighed 35 pounds (16 kg).

LEE ENFIELD .303 RIFLES

Lee Enfield rifles were used mainly by British forces. They used 10-cartridge magazines. The rifle weighed 8.7 pounds (3.9 kg).

HANDGUNS AND EDGED WEAPONS

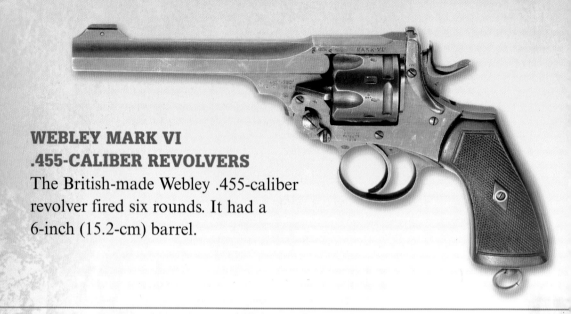

WEBLEY MARK VI
.455-CALIBER REVOLVERS

The British-made Webley .455-caliber
revolver fired six rounds. It had a
6-inch (15.2-cm) barrel.

STEYR 9-MM AUTOMATIC PISTOLS

The Steyr pistol was the official handgun of
the Austro-Hungarian and Romanian armies.
Its magazine held eight rounds.

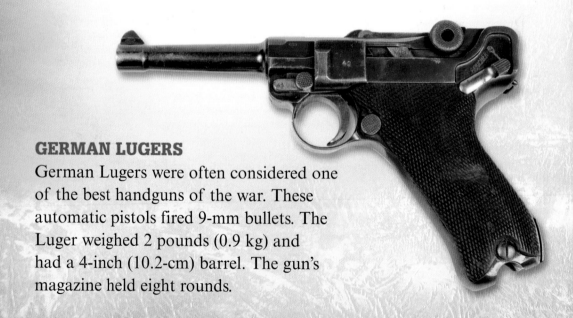

GERMAN LUGERS

German Lugers were often considered one
of the best handguns of the war. These
automatic pistols fired 9-mm bullets. The
Luger weighed 2 pounds (0.9 kg) and
had a 4-inch (10.2-cm) barrel. The gun's
magazine held eight rounds.

M1911 PISTOLS

The Browning-Colt Model 1911 was used mainly by U.S. forces. The pistol weighed 2 pounds (0.9 kg) and had a 5-inch (12.7-cm) barrel. Its magazine held seven rounds.

GERMAN BAYONETS

The German double-edged bayonet was 10.25 inches (26 cm) long. It weighed 0.5 pound (0.23 kg) and was made to fit onto the Mauser Gewehr 1898 rifle. Many German soldiers used these bayonets while fighting in hand-to-hand combat. The blades were not official German army weapons, but soldiers were still allowed to use them.

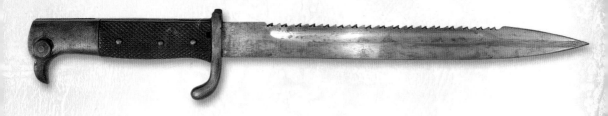

RUSSIAN MODEL 1907 TROOPER DAGGERS

Russian trooper daggers had carved handles. The blades were more than 17 inches (43 cm) long. Some Russian troops fought with these daggers instead of bayonets.

GRENADES, TRENCH CLUBS, AND FLAMETHROWERS

Grenades, flamethrowers, and clubs were important in trench warfare. Grenades came in many shapes and sizes. They could look like lightbulbs, lemons, apples, or even discs. Allied soldiers used grenades that looked like small pineapples. By the end of the war, Britain had produced at least 75,000,000 grenades.

GERMAN STICK GRENADE

Because of their appearance, German stick grenades were often called "potato mashers." This weapon had a fuse loaded into its hollow handle that could be lit by pulling a cord.

BATTLE FACT

About 1.5 billion shells were fired on the Western Front. French farmers are still finding unexploded grenades and shells in the ground today.

BRITISH MILLS GRENADES

The British used different models of the Mills grenade. These early grenades were very dangerous. The Mills Mark II often exploded in the hand of the thrower. In 1916 accidents were reduced when soldiers began using the Mark III.

TRENCH CLUBS

Hand-to-hand combat in the trenches was brutal. Trench clubs were often handmade weapons. Soldiers made them from various materials like nails, spikes, and metal rods. The clubs were used during night raids on enemy trenches.

FLAMETHROWERS

Flamethrowers used a mix of oil and gasoline that was shot out under pressure. The flamethrower could blast fire for two minutes at a distance of 60 feet (18.3 m). Flamethrowers were first used in combat on February 26, 1915. The Germans used them against French forces near Verdun, France.

World War I saw the first regular use of many heavy weapons and combat vehicles. These heavy weapons were capable of causing mass destruction on a scale never seen before.

MACHINE GUNS AND HEAVY FIELD GUNS

75 MM FIELD GUNS

These heavy field guns weighed 2,657 pounds (1,205 kg). They could fire 16-pound (7.3-kg) shells more than 4 miles (6.4 kilometers). The gun normally fired six rounds per minute. But when needed, it could fire up to 20 rounds per minute. The gun was used at the Battle of the Marne to stop German advances in France.

HOTCHKISS MACHINE GUNS

Hotchkiss guns were the only air-cooled, gas-operated heavy machine guns in the war. They weighed 52 pounds (24 kg) and were often used as anti-aircraft weapons. The United States used the Hotchkiss more than its own Browning machine gun.

BRITISH MARK I 60-POUNDER FIELD GUNS

The Mark I was Britain's largest field gun. A team of horses was required to pull it into position. It fired 60-pound (27-kg) shells at targets nearly 6 miles (9.7 km) away. The British used the Mark I at the Battle of the Somme.

BIG BERTHA

Big Bertha was a 420 mm howitzer. The German gun weighed 75 tons (68 metric tons) and had a crew of 280 soldiers. The giant gun could fire shells weighing 2,052 pounds (931 kg) at targets up to 9 miles (14.5 km) away.

GERMAN MAXIM MG 08 MACHINE GUNS

German Maxim MG 08 machine guns weighed 36 pounds (16.3 kg) and had a 2.6-foot (0.8-m) long barrels. These guns could fire up to 500 rounds per minute. The barrel was covered with a cooling jacket that held 5 pints (2.4 liters) of water to help keep the barrel cool.

TANKS

When Britain began using tanks in battle, it changed the course of the war. The first tank assault happened on September 15, 1916, between the Somme and Ancre Rivers in France. The Allies' tanks surprised about 300 German troops in their trenches and forced them to surrender.

BRITISH MARK I

Mark I tanks came in two versions. The "male" was armed with two 6-pound (2.7-kg) guns and four machine guns. The "female" had seven machine guns. They each carried a crew of eight.

BRITISH MARK IV

The Mark IV tank could reach speeds of 3.5 miles (5.6 km) per hour. It had 57 mm guns, and 0.5-inch (1.3-cm) thick armor. Mark IV tanks were used at Cambrai, France, on November 20, 1917.

THE WHIPPET

The British Whippet tank had a gun **turret** at the rear, and it carried four Hotchkiss machine guns. Its two engines each powered one of the tank's tracks. The Whippet was small enough to be operated by a single soldier in an emergency.

 turret—a rotating structure on top of a military vehicle that holds a weapon

GERMAN A7V TANKS

Germany's A7V tank was the only German-made tank in the war. It was armed with six heavy machine guns and a 57 mm cannon. The A7V took part in the first tank-against-tank battle of the war on April 24, 1918.

FRENCH SCHNEIDER TANKS

The Schneider was armed with one 75 mm gun and two Hotchkiss machine guns. These French tanks were first used in battle on April 16, 1917, at the beginning of the Nivelle Offensive in France.

RENAULT FT-17 TANKS

The French Renault FT-17 was the first tank with a turret that could turn around in a full circle. This design allowed the tank's two-man crew to fire in any direction.

SHIPS

Battleships existed long before World War I broke out. But warships greatly improved in size and firepower during the course of the war. The war also saw the birth of the naval aircraft carrier.

HMS DREADNOUGHT

The British warship HMS *Dreadnought* was armed with 12-inch (30.5-cm) guns mounted on twin turrets. It also carried 24 12-pound guns. The ship's success led the British navy to create the Dreadnought class warships.

SMS NASSAU

Germany built its own Dreadnought class battleships. The SMS *Nassau* was one of the first. It had twelve 11-inch (28-cm), twelve 5.9-inch (15-cm), and sixteen 3.4-inch (8.6-cm) guns. The *Nassau* entered the war in 1914. On May 31, 1916, the *Nassau* crashed into the British destroyer *Spitfire*, causing great damage and nearly destroying the British ship.

HMS QUEEN ELIZABETH

The HMS *Queen Elizabeth* was a super-dreadnaught class ship that carried a crew of 1,016. It carried eight 15-inch (38-cm) guns, twelve 6-inch (15-cm) guns, and twelve 12-pounders. The ship's armor was 13 inches (33 cm) thick. The *Queen Elizabeth* fought in the Mediterranean and North Seas.

BRITISH M-1 SUBMARINES

British M class submarines were 300 feet (91 m) long. They were armed with four 18-inch (46-cm) torpedo tubes. M-1 subs also carried a 12-inch (31-cm) gun. The sub fired an 850-pound (386-kg) shell that had to be loaded while on the water's surface.

GERMAN U-19 CLASS SUBMARINES

This diesel-powered submarine could travel about 4,000 miles (6,437 km) before refueling. A U-19 sub was responsible for sinking the British passenger ship RMS *Lusitania*. The U-19 carried four torpedo tubes and one 2-inch (5-cm) gun. It had a crew of 28 men.

AIRPLANES

Along with tanks and heavy guns, World War I also saw the first widespread use of airplanes in battle. The first military airplanes carried few weapons and only flew 50 to 75 miles (80 to 121 km) per hour. But by 1917, military airplanes were heavily armed with machine guns. They could also reach speeds of about 150 miles (240 km) per hour.

FOKKER DR-1

This German triplane was a favorite of German pilot Baron Manfred von Richthofen. The Fokker DR-1 could fly nearly 4 miles (6 km) high and up to 115 miles (185 km) per hour. Also known as the "Red Baron," Richthofen earned his nickname from his bright red plane. He painted it red so enemy pilots would know who shot them down.

BRITISH SOPWITH CAMELS

British Sopwith Camels had twin Vickers machine guns and could reach 122 miles (196 km) per hour. Some historians believe a Camel was responsible for shooting down Germany's famous "Red Baron" pilot on April 21, 1918.

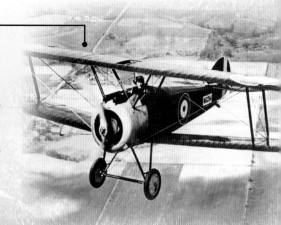

BRISTOL F2B

The British-built Bristol F2B was armed with one fixed Vickers machine gun. It also carried one or two free-moving Lewis guns and twelve 20-pound (9-kg) bombs.

ALBATROS DIII

The German-built Albatross DIII was armed with two Spandau machine guns. The Albatross could reach speeds of 103 miles (166 km) per hour and could fly as high as 3.4 miles (5.5 km).

SPAD S XIII

The Spad S XIII was a French biplane fighter armed with two Vickers guns. It could fly up to 4 miles (6.6 km) high and as fast as 138 miles (222 km) per hour. Ace American pilot Eddie Rickenbacker flew a Spad for part of the war.

GLOSSARY

assassination (uh-sass-uh-NAY-shuhn)—the murder of someone who is well known or important

howitzer (HOW-uht-sur)—a long-barreled cannon that fires shells long distances

magazine (MAG-uh-zeen)—a metal or plastic case that holds bullets and fits inside a gun

puttee (PUHT-ee)—a strip of cloth wound around a soldier's leg from ankle to knee as part of a uniform

shell (SHEL)—a metal container filled with gunpowder and fired from a large gun

shrapnel (SHRAP-nuhl)—pieces of metal that have broken off of an explosive shell

torpedo tube (tor-PEE-doh TOOB)—a tube-like structure on a submarine from which explosive torpedos are launched

trench (TRENCH)—a long, deep area dug into the ground with dirt piled up on one side for defense

turret (TUR-it)—a rotating, armored structure that holds a weapon on top of a military vehicle

READ MORE

Adams, Simon. *World War I*. DK Eyewitness Books. New York: DK Pub., 2007.

Perritano, John. *World War I*. America at War. New York: Franklin Watts, 2010.

Turner, Jason. *World War I, 1914–1918*. Wars Day by Day. Redding, Conn.: Brown Bear Books, 2009.

INTERNET SITES

FactHound offers a safe, fun way to find Internet sites related to this book. All of the sites on FactHound have been researched by our staff.

Here's all you do:

Visit *www.facthound.com*

Type in this code: 9781429676496

 Super-cool stuff! Check out projects, games and lots more at **www.capstonekids.com**

INDEX